GW00503817

MONSTERS, INC.
The Office:
A Survival Guide

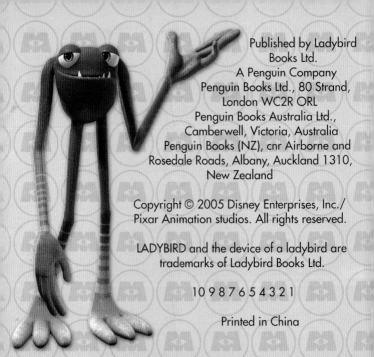

Published by Ladybird
Books Ltd.
A Penguin Company
Penguin Books Ltd., 80 Strand,
London WC2R ORL
Penguin Books Australia Ltd.,
Camberwell, Victoria, Australia
Penguin Books (NZ), cnr Airborne and
Rosedale Roads, Albany, Auckland 1310,
New Zealand

LADYBIRD and the device of a ladybird are
trademarks of Ladybird Books Ltd.

10 9 8 7 6 5 4 3 2 1

Printed in China

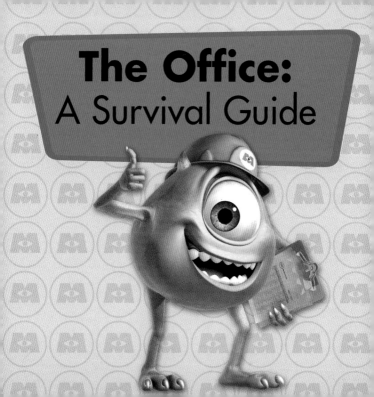

The Office:
A Survival Guide

MONSTERS, INC.

WE SCARE BECAUSE WE CARE

Hi Guys!

The Welfare Committee thought we should put together some sort of guide to help out you newbies. Work can be pretty scary sometimes, after all. Today's hapless employee can have to deal with monstrous co-workers, sneaky bosses with their own secret agendas and the constant fear of redundancy as the company struggles to survive. Hopefully we can help you cope.

And it ain't all bad. The coffee's always hot and sludgy, the hours are okay and there's always the chance of office romance...

Sulley   MIKE

Your dedicated authors —
a gorgeous hunk* and a
weird-looking guy

*with one eye

Henry J. Waternoose III has got several of his eyes on you

Re: KNOW YOUR BOSS
Five common types

THE JELLYFISH Easygoing, soft, flexible; but also indecisive and liable to collapse under pressure.

THE COBRA Beautiful, smooth, smart; but has a sharp tongue, is hypnotic and poisonous.

THE LIZARD Cool, unemotional, calm and slow-moving; can bite or fall apart if over-stressed.

THE SILVERBACK GORILLA Throws weight around, yells a lot, flares nostrils. Doesn't actually do any work — not that bright.

THE PUPPY Sweet, young, enthusiastic, fun to be with. Warning: may pee all over you and run away.

Re: STEER CLEAR
Monsters to avoid at work

PRAISE HOOVER Collects all the compliments floating about, regardless of the intended recipient.

CHAOS MAGNET Sucks weirdness and irrelevancy into their orbit without meaning to. Makes work more interesting, if unpredictable and a bit scary.

GRAVITY WELL Makes everything seem really, really heavy. A three-hour meeting with a Gravity Well feels like several lifetimes.

INVERSE MIDAS Everything they touch turns to trash. Don't let them get their tentacles on your work.

EMOTIONAL SPONGE Big, wet and prone to leaking uncontrollably when pushed.

Randall Boggs is one of those guys you need to watch out for – which can be tricky in his case

Look, I was anxious and in a hurry. Not scared, right?

Re: LEAVING TIME
Five signs of a sinking ship (so make like a rat)

- Chair older than you. Computer screen has green lettering on a black background.
- Milk bill not paid. Cleaning staff laid off. Infestations of vermin.
- Friday night drinks to say goodbye to laid-off staff. Every week.
- Colleagues openly writing CVs and applying for new jobs at their desks.
- Boss invests the employee pension scheme in his own private company.

Re: THE LOVE BOAT IS ABOUT TO SET SAIL
Spotting secret office affairs

- Smiling and blushing at emails. 'Oh, it's, it's … nothing.' (Said while deleting furiously.)
- Phone calls ended the instant anyone else enters the room.
- Both monsters arriving within three minutes of each other. Every day.
- Lo-n-n-n-g trips 'to the stationery cupboard.' Taking the scenic route past a certain workstation.
- Reasons miraculously appear that necessitate them working together. On a 'Special Project'.
- Conferences and training days are arranged in far-off locations.

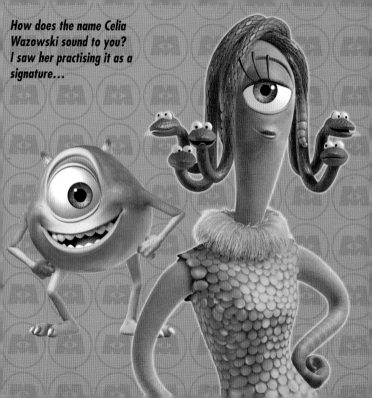

How does the name Celia Wazowski sound to you? I saw her practising it as a signature...

These kids are Needleman (right) and Smitty (left), but to be honest they're kinda similar

Re: YOU DON'T HAVE TO LIKE THEM
But you have to make them like you – or else

PAYROLL CLERK *'Oh, did it not go through? You'd better give me your account details. Again.'*

SECURITY GUARD *'I don't care, you have to show a valid pass or wait for someone to come down and vouch for you.'*

POSTROOM SLUG *'Nah, nothing for you. Again.'*

RECEPTIONIST *'Oh, did you not want to speak to them? They seemed very angry so I thought it was important.'*

Re: HEALTH AND SAFETY: NOT BORING, HONEST

It's never been the most exciting aspect of work — be honest, have you read any of that big poster in the kitchen? — but it needs to be taken seriously.

If you get issued with a hard hat, wear it — you never know when an evil co-worker will hurl a piece of equipment at you.

And a stray sock might seem pretty insignificant, but in some places it counts as a 23-19, and requires a full-scale clean-up by monsters in yellow suits. You could end up getting forcibly shaved. All over. In public.

The CDA guys like to go scubadiving with vacuum cleaners when they're not at work

Now you see him, now you don't.
How can you trust a guy like that?

Re: HOW TO IDENTIFY A GHOST BOSS

Ghost bosses are heard but never seen; they only communicate indirectly, by memo and email. They have representatives on Earth who do their bidding (secretaries), but who refuse to help you to actually make contact.

Very rarely you may see one flit silently through your building, but your fellow monsters won't believe you.

Because ghost bosses are so disconnected from reality, they only care about the appearance of office life, not the actual work being done in it. All their memos are about Tidiness and Punctuality (the lack of).

Re: THERE ARE THOSE WHO WORK, AND THOSE WHO PAPERWORK

Paperwork stinks. You don't understand it, you don't enjoy it but you still have to do it. And it means you have to deal with the scariest monster in the office.

They have all the power because they DO understand paperwork, and maybe even enjoy it. They certainly seem to enjoy your distress and discomfort; it's like being a traffic warden, only drier.

The only really successful strategies to keep paperwork at bay are:

- Doing a little every day rather than letting it pile up.
- Passing it on for someone else to deal with.

I'm sure Roz is really beautiful on the inside. Really deep down inside...

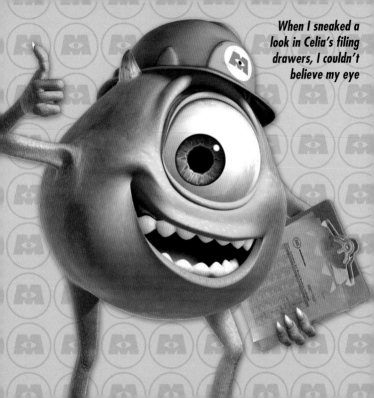

When I sneaked a look in Celia's filing drawers, I couldn't believe my eye

Re: *FUN WITH FILING CABINETS*

Filing: no one ever checks it, and no one ever chucks it (I once found competition entries from 1956 filling a four-drawer cabinet). So use that big metal box to hide something far more useful – just keep the key secret…

- *Snacks cabinet – sweeties in the bottom, savoury nibbles in the middle, refreshing drinks in the top. Boss goes home = party time!*
- *Entertainment centre: CD player, speakers, glitter ball, disco lights.*
- *Home from home: sleeping bag, change of clothes, toothbrush. For when you miss the last bus home.*

Re: *GOTTA GETTA WORK*

Confused about your commuting options?
This summarises your choices.

	FOR	AGAINST
BUS	Cheap	Greasy head marks on the windows
CAR	Private	Slow, expensive
TRAIN	You can fall asleep	Ditto plus other people's sweat
ON FOOT	Very cheap	Slow, tiring
BIKE	Cheap, good exercise	Sweaty nylon shorts, makes you smug

I'm pretty attached to my car, but Sulley prefers to stalk

Top tip: don't upset a girlfriend whose hair can bite you

Re: BYE BYE LOVE
Spotting the end of a relationship

- Angry typing of increasingly sarcastic emails.
- Storming out of meetings in which each other's work is 'subtly' criticised.
- All communication becomes non-verbal, even though they sit two metres apart.
- One arranges a three-week solo research trip for the other — to Helsingborg and Hull — in November.

Re: *TO ALL EMPLOYEES*
Emails you don't need

'I will be out of the office for the next hour.'

'The IT department will be working on upgrading non-critical LAN subroutines this weekend. You should not experience any noticeable change in server activity.'

'Has anyone found my head-lice comb?'

'Felicity Complete-Stranger has been promoted to Assistant Archivist, in recognition of her sterling work over the last year as Archival Assistant. I am sure you will join me in congratulating her.'

Fungus is insecure, lonely and very bright – ideal accomplice material

Bile (Phlegm to his friends) was never that convincing as a Scarer for some reason

Re: *NAFF DESK DECORATIONS*

- *Multiple cute models of pigs, cats or sheep but especially frogs.*
- *A large photo in a large gilt frame of your large family, grinning in their Sunday best, against a soft-focus brown swirly background.*
- *Computer-generated certificate congratulating you on completing a routine training course.*
- *Photocopy of any part of your anatomy.*
- *Inspirational poster of an eagle at sunset over a mountain with a slogan like 'Be All That You Can Be.'*
- *Signed photo of a politician.*

Re: **SAVE CASH – LIVE IN THE OFFICE**

This is easier than you'd think. I knew an estate agent who lived in the houses he was meant to be selling for six months.

- Keep it discreet; no sitting at your desk in your pyjamas eating cornflakes or leaving underwear on radiators to dry.
- Find a quiet filing cabinet or cupboard for all your stuff. Don't get it delivered by a removals van.
- Find a nearby launderette or dry-cleaners. Wearing the same outfit for more than three days is a giveaway.
- You should 'leave' and 'arrive' at unremarkable times, so you need to get friendly with the security guard (I never said it was THAT easy).

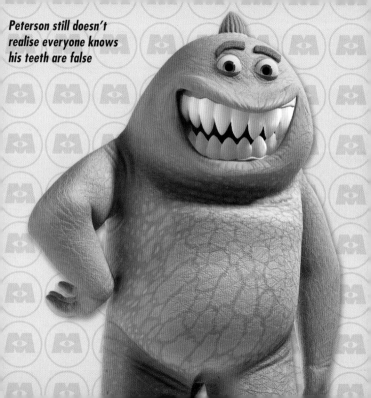

Peterson still doesn't realise everyone knows his teeth are false

Re: *YOUR COMPUTER HATES YOU*

It's a little-known fact that office monsters give off odourless invisible pheromones when they are stressed.

It's even less well-known that there are critical components within sophisticated electronic equipment that are sensitive to these pheromones and start to function erratically in their presence. To put it another way: they can smell your fear.

How else can you explain the printer suddenly failing when you absolutely HAVE to get that report out in the next hour?

Re: *URBAN MYTHS FOR COMMUTERS*

- Mobile phone technology means no one standing near you can hear what you say; so swear and shout as much as you like.
- No one in a train carriage can smell your body odour. Or your silent farts.
- Everyone really loves your taste in music. Wind the window down and turn it up.
- Anything from your mouth (spit, gum, kebabs) ceases to exist the instant you spit it out.
- It may not look like it, but all cars have one-way glass in the windows. So no one can see you picking your nose.

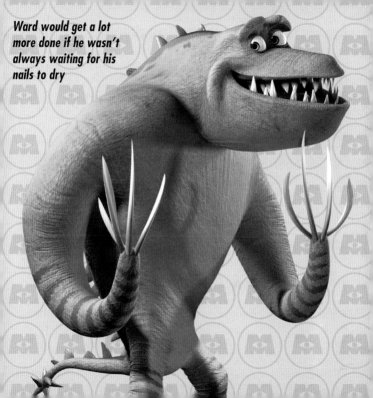

Ward would get a lot
more done if he wasn't
always waiting for his
nails to dry

For a little guy Mike has big dreams. Maybe he should drink less coffee

Re: GETTING OUT
Should you go freelance?

Staying as an employee

FOR:
- All the paperclips you can steal
- Possibility of snogs at Christmas party

AGAINST:
- Pointless meetings
- No respect or power
- Commuting
- Irritating co-workers

Working for yourself

FOR:
- You can work in your underwear/ in the garden/ down the cafe

AGAINST:
- No sick pay or pension
- No IT department, receptionist or tea slug
- Far too easy to slack off

Re: *OBSOLESCENCE CORNER*

If you still use more than two of these, your office is officially a World Heritage Museum.

- ☐ Dial telephone
- ☐ Typewriter
- ☐ Ashtray (smoking allowed at desk)
- ☐ Carbon paper
- ☐ Wooden desk or chair
- ☐ Filofax
- ☐ Floppy disks
- ☐ Thermal fax paper that goes black in sunlight
- ☐ Answering machine with a cassette tape in it
- ☐ Computer more than three years old

Creepy thought: the two oldest folk in your office may have had a fling in their youth

Ricky is an easy-going guy – unless you touch his toothbrush. Ever seen an angry coffee table?

Re: LINES YOU DON'T WANT TO HEAR AT THE OFFICE PARTY

'I've got my pulling knickers on. Look!'

'Owing to difficult trading conditions the party for staff has been cancelled. Directors will have their seasonal lunch as usual.'

'Happy Christmas, here's your P45.'

'You know, I've always respected the work you've done for me. I think you could go far in this company, if you, ah, play your cards right...'

'Your voucher entitles you to one free drink, after which there will be a pay bar.'

Re: SPOTTING AN EVIL CO-WORKER

They start small: nicking your stapler, 'borrowing' the departmental laptop for nine months. Stamp out this behaviour, otherwise it will escalate. Watch for the signs:

- Regular work neglected; deadlines missed.
- Suddenly spend lots of time with geeky hench-monsters with useful technical skills.
- Furtive meetings held in toilets, with hissed orders and chest-tapping.
- Spotted wheeling crates with mysterious contents.
- Repeated visits to obscure, unused areas of the building — where they can never be found.
- The power surges and fades, to the accompaniment of maniacal laughter.

I don't know, foil a guy's dastardly plot and all of a sudden he goes off on one

George Sanderson stays pretty cheery, despite having had a shaving rash over his entire body